DIANA

Her True Story –

In Her Own Words

DIANA

Her True Story – *In Her Own Words*

Completely Revised Edition

ANDREW MORTON

MICHAEL O'MARA BOOKS LIMITED

First published in 1992
as *Diana, Her True Story* by
Michael O'Mara Books Limited
9 Lion Yard, Tremadoc Road,
London SW4 7NQ

This revised edition
first published in Great Britain in 1997
by Michael O'Mara Books Limited

A CIP catalogue record for this book is available
from the British Library

ISBN 1-85479-270-9

3 5 7 9 10 8 6 4

Designed and typeset by Martin Bristow

Printed and bound by Clays Limited, St Ives plc

Contents

Acknowledgments 7

Foreword 9

In Her Own Words 23

1 ***'I Was Supposed To Be a Boy'*** 70

2 ***'Just Call Me "Sir"'*** 95

3 ***'Such Hope in My Heart'*** 119

4 ***'My Cries for Help'*** 132

5 ***'Darling, I'm About To Disappear'*** 148

6 ***'My Life Has Changed Its Course'*** 159

7 ***'I Don't Rattle Their Cages'*** 177

8 ***'I Did My Best'*** 202

9 ***'We'd Run Out of Steam'*** 213

10 ***'My Acting Career Is Over'*** 226

11	***'I Am Going To Be Me'***	241
12	***'Tell Me Yes'***	255
13	***The People's Princess***	270
	Index	284

Acknowledgments

This biography of the Princess of Wales is unique in that the story contained in its pages would never have appeared had it not been for the wholehearted co-operation of Diana, Princess of Wales. The story is based on lengthy, tape-recorded interviews with Diana, supplemented by the testimony of her family and friends. Like Diana, they spoke with honesty and frankness in spite of the fact it meant laying aside the ingrained habits of discretion and loyalty which proximity to royalty invariably engenders. My thanks for their co-operation are therefore all the more heartfelt and sincere.

My grateful thanks, too, to the Princess of Wales's brother, the 9th Earl Spencer for his insights and reminiscences, particularly about the Princess's childhood and teenage years.

My thanks also to the Baroness Falkender, Carolyn Bartholomew, Sue Beechey, Dr James Colthurst, James Gilbey, Malcolm Groves, Lucinda Craig Harvey, Peter and Neil Hickling, Felix Lyle, Michael Nash, Delissa Needham, Adam Russell, Rory Scott, Angela Serota, Muriel Stevens, Oonagh Toffolo and Stephen Twigg.

There are others whose positions prevent me from officially acknowledging their assistance. Their unstinting guidance has been invaluable.

My thanks to my publisher, Michael O'Mara for his guidance and support on the tortuous path from conception to completion, and to my wife Lynne for her patience and forbearance.

Andrew Morton
September 1997

Photograph Acknowledgments

Before his death in March 1992, the father of the Princess of Wales, the 8th Earl Spencer very kindly allowed access to his private family photograph albums. Many of the photographs in this volume are reproduced from those albums. His generous co-operation is greatly appreciated.

The beautiful, modern portraits of the Princess of Wales and her children which appear in this book are all by Patrick Demarchelier. The sources of all other photographs in this volume are stated in the captions.

Foreword

THE TRAGIC DEATH OF DIANA, Princess of Wales on 31 August 1997 plunged the world into paroxysms of grief, despair and regret, unrivalled in the modern era. This spontaneous eruption of anguish was a sign not only of her enormous personal impact on the world stage but of the potency of her position, of what she represented as a woman and as a flag-bearer for a new generation, a new order and a new future. Even now we are still trying to come to terms not only with her loss but with what she meant to us, why those who never met her felt moved to a depth of grief that they would not display even for their own kith and kin. By some indefinable alchemy she had come to embody the spirit of the age, so that when we buried her we also laid to rest something of ourselves. Those who came in pilgrimage to lay flowers at Kensington Palace, her London home, wept not just for her but for themselves. Ironically, she was once asked what she would want as an epitaph on her grave. 'A great hope crushed in its infancy,' was her reply, a phrase that unwittingly captured not only her short life but the spirit she represented.

Amid the tears and the flowers, there was guilt, shame and anger at the royal family who abandoned her and at the mass media who hounded her. The mood ran much deeper, demonstrating how far the temper of the times had changed; the tectonic plates which underpin society having shifted culturally, socially and politically in the previous few years. Just as the people had spoken in the elections of May 1997 which gave the Labour Party a historic landslide victory, so in the days before and during Diana's funeral they voiced their collective displeasure and disappointment at two other mighty, but unaccountable, institutions, the media and the monarchy, whom they believed had betrayed the wishes not only of Diana, Princess of Wales, but of themselves. She was of the people and for the people, and the Prime

Minister, Tony Blair captured that sentiment when he described her as 'the people's princess'.

When the Queen, standing at the gates of Buckingham Palace with her family, bowed her head to the gun carriage carrying Diana's coffin it was far more than a gesture of respect for a much-loved woman. It was also an acknowledgment of the passing of the old order, the ascendancy of a new ethic which Diana so vividly personified. In his electrifying funeral oration Diana's brother, Earl Spencer caught that mood; in just seven short minutes transforming himself from a little-known sprig of the aristocracy to a national hero. More important than his rapier thrusts at the royal family – 'she needed no royal title to continue to generate her particular brand of magic' – and his more bludgeoning attack on the media, was the fact that his eulogy, both in delivery and sentiment, so clearly captured the spirit of Diana. Courageous, reckless, cherishing honesty and truth above the social niceties, cock-eyed in its logic, his address achieved what Diana had been struggling for throughout her adult life: to speak to the people over the heads of those who rule us, be they the royal family, politicians or the press barons. As the spontaneous applause following his oration showed, in her death Diana had found her champion.

In the coming months, years and decades following a momentous week in the life not only of Britain, but of the world, much will be written and discussed about just what Diana meant to us as individuals and collectively as a society. As her life truly represented a parable of our times, this is not only right and proper but eminently desirable. At the same time there will be a necessary evaluation of her life; even as I write there are dozens of biographies, videos and commemorative albums under way. This, too, is inevitable, for we want to know about the personal attributes which propelled Diana into becoming a figure of such mythic proportions. In time the silt of history will cloud her memory; the memoirs of those who knew her, or thought they knew her, filtering and shifting the public's perception of a woman who has become the most cherished icon of the modern era. There is an enduring danger that Diana's perception of her life, an account she was so desperate to tell, will be obscured and revised with the passage of the decades.

It would be easy for me to subscribe to that process: both my books, *Diana, Her True Story* and *Diana, Her New Life* are currently bestsellers around the world so there is every commercial imperative to allow any distortions within their pages to remain. This, however, would be to dishonour her memory, to distort history and to run counter to the people's spirit of honesty and openness so eloquently captured by her brother, Earl Spencer at her funeral.

For what people have never realized is the extent of the Princess's commitment to my book, *Diana, Her True Story*, which was first published in June 1992. To all intents and purposes it was her autobiography, the personal testament of a woman who saw herself at the time as voiceless and powerless. The story contained in its pages came from her lips, the pain and heartache in her life revealed in a series of tape-recorded interviews at Kensington Palace during the summer and autumn of 1991. There were no camera lights, no rehearsals, no second takes. Her words came from the heart, outlining in graphic and, at times, agonizing detail the sorrow and loneliness felt by a woman admired and adored around the world. Given the unfolding tragedy of her life and her untimely death, it is hard not to re-read and listen again to her words without shedding a tear. Today her testimony stands as an eloquent and unique witness before the tribunal of history.

So much has changed since that fateful summer of 1991 that it is difficult to convey the mood of impotent suffocation then felt by the Princess of Wales. She considered herself to be a prisoner trapped inside a bitterly unfulfilled marriage, shackled to an unsympathetic royal system and chained to a wholly unrealistic public image of her life. Everywhere she went she was followed by a bodyguard, her every movement was logged while each visitor to her home was noted and checked. She believed she was under constant surveillance, not only monitored by police and photographers, but watched with suspicion by the royal family and their courtiers. All the while she nursed a secret, a secret that was slowly but surely gnawing away at her. As far as she was concerned her life was a grotesque and implacable lie.

Her marriage to the Prince of Wales was effectively over. She knew that he had returned to the first love of his life, Camilla Parker-Bowles. Yet, like a character in a Kafka novel, her concerns were dismissed as so much fantasy and paranoia by an Establishment that went to elaborate lengths to conceal the infidelities of her husband. As Diana was to explain years later in her famous television interview on the BBC's *Panorama*: 'Friends on my husband's side were indicating that I was again unstable, sick and should be put in a home of some sort in order to get better. I was almost an embarrassment.' As the world now knows her instincts proved true, the Prince of Wales himself having confessed to adultery after his marriage had 'irretrievably broken down' during the mid-1980s.

At the time, as she watched her marriage unravelling, her greatest fear was that her husband's circle would soon begin the process of discrediting her and convincing the world that she was irrational – unfit either for motherhood or to represent the monarchy.

However, the frustration that seethed inside her lay as much with an antiquated royal system as with her fading marriage. Intuitively she felt that the style of the monarchy was outdated, while her own role and ambitions were continually being circumscribed. The courtiers, or the 'men in grey suits' as she called them, were happy if she were viewed as a dutiful wife and mother, an attractive adornment to her intellectual husband. At the same time, as far as she was concerned the system was constantly chipping away at her position in order to bolster Prince Charles's popularity.

As she looked out from her lonely prison, rarely a day passed without the sound of another cell door slamming, another lock snapping shut as the fiction of the fairytale was further embellished in the public's mind. The publication in 1991 of a series of books and articles celebrating the couple's 10th wedding anniversary served to weld new bars to her jail. 'She felt the lid was closing in on her,' a friend recalled. 'Unlike other women, she did not have the freedom to leave with her children.'

Like a prisoner condemned for a crime she did not commit, Diana had a crying need to tell the world the truth about her life, the distress she felt and the ambitions she nurtured. Her sense of injustice was profound. Quite simply, she wanted the liberty to speak her mind, the opportunity to tell people the whole story of her life and to let them judge her accordingly. She felt somehow that if she was able to explain her story to the people, her people, they could truly understand her before it was too late. 'Let them be my judge,' she said, confident that her public would not criticize her as harshly as the royal family or the mass media. Her desire to explain what she saw as the truth of her case was matched by a nagging fear that at any moment her enemies in the Palace would have her classified as mentally ill and locked away. This was no idle fear – when her *Panorama* interview was screened in 1995, the then Armed Forces Minister,

Nicholas Soames, a close friend and former equerry to Prince Charles, described her as displaying 'the advanced stages of paranoia'.

How then could she smuggle her message to the outside world? Reviewing Britain's social landscape she saw that there were few outlets for her story. For even today, though wounded and humbled, the monarchy exerts a powerful and compelling influence over the mass media. Just six years ago, as *Diana, Her True Story* was being prepared, the royal family's ascendancy was almost total; the House of Windsor was then, even more than now, the most influential and feared family in the land. Credible media outlets, the BBC, ITV and the so-called quality newspapers, would have had a collective attack of the vapours if she had signalled that she wanted them to publish the truth of her position. Again, if her story had appeared in the tabloid press it would have been dismissed by the Establishment as so much exaggerated rubbish.

So what to do? Within her small circle of intimate friends there was sufficient alarm for several to fear for Diana's safety. It was known that she had made a number of half-hearted suicide attempts in the past and, as her desperation grew, there were genuine fears that she could take her own life; worries tempered by a balancing belief that ultimately her love for her children could never take her down that path.

In the winter of 1990, when I first started researching a biography of the Princess of Wales, I knew little of these concerns. As both a journalist and author I had been writing about the royal family since 1982, the year after Diana's marriage to the Prince of Wales, and had built up a number of contacts inside the various palaces and in the circles of the Princess of Wales and the Duchess of York. Earlier in 1990 I had written *Diana's Diary*, a lifestyle book about the Princess which, I was later to learn, had been well-received by her.

During my researches for this book it became clear that all was not well with the royal marriage, Diana's friends and former members of staff making dark hints about the Princess's unhappiness. While these allusions were intriguing, they were nothing new. Speculation about the Waleses' marriage had been growing ever since a visit to Portugal in 1987 during which they had insisted on staying in separate suites. For my latest book, a full-scale biography of the Princess, I set about trying to uncover the facts surrounding Diana's life. I was soon to learn the painful truth.

Meanwhile, as Diana continued to consider the dilemma of her life inside the royal family, she noticed that a series of articles I had written for the *Sunday Times*, notably on the furore over Prince Charles's offer of a party at Highgrove for her 30th birthday as well as the departure of the Prince's private secretary, Sir Christopher Airey, were sympathetic to her cause. She was now aware that I was piecing together her life story, that I was an independent writer, neither wedded to Fleet Street nor, more importantly, in the thrall of Buckingham Palace – issues of some importance as she considered her future course of action. In any event, after some initial and expected hesitation, she decided to unlock the door to the inner sanctum of her psyche. I was asked to become the conduit of her true story.

There was one major stumbling block. The arrival of an author at the gates of Kensington Palace would immediately set alarm bells ringing – especially as Prince Charles was still in residence. Just as Martin Bashir, the television journalist who later interviewed the Princess for the BBC *Panorama* programme, was to discover, subterfuge was the only way to circumvent an ever-vigilant royal system. In November 1995, when he conducted his interview, he smuggled his BBC camera crew into Kensington Palace on a quiet Sunday.

For my part Diana was interviewed by proxy, using a trusted intermediary so that if the Princess was asked: 'Did you meet Andrew Morton?' she could answer with a resounding 'NO'. I submitted endless written questions about every aspect of her life, starting, naturally, with her childhood. In return she answered as best she could, speaking into a rather ancient tape recorder in the quiet of her private sitting room. While it was an imperfect method which gave no opportunity for immediate follow-up questions, very quickly a picture emerged of a life which was totally at variance with the accepted image. As a writer who had spent much of his life working in a royal world where evasion, equivocation and secrecy were the official currency, at first I was stunned by Diana's candour and disbelieving of the astonishing story she revealed. In the first interview session, although lots of questions had been prepared beforehand, once the tape recorder was switched on her words spilled out of her, almost without interruption and with her barely pausing for breath. It was a great release.

For the first time in her royal life she felt empowered. At last her voice was about to be heard, the truth was about to be told. 'Tell

Noah [her nickname for me] to make sure the story gets out,' she would say to trusted confidants, disappointed that the process of writing and researching a book could not happen overnight. Her choice of nickname revealed something about her gentle sense of humour. It had arisen after I was described in an American newspaper as a 'notable author and historian'. She was tickled by such a pompous depiction and from then on always used the acronym, Noah, when referring to me. It became a running joke.

In some respects her exhilaration at unburdening herself of her secret was little different from that of others who have emerged from an institution which exists, almost by definition, by a mixture of myth and magic. Over the years I have interviewed numerous former royal employees who have felt a sense of relief that at last they were able to tell the story of what life is really like inside Buckingham Palace. It is a form of confession. 'I was at the end of my tether. I was desperate,' Diana argued during her *Panorama* interview. 'I think I was so fed up with being seen as someone who was a basket case because I am a very strong person and I know that causes complications in the system that I live in.'

For Diana, however, the act of talking about her life provoked many memories, some cheerful, others almost too difficult to put into words. Like a gust of wind across a field of corn, her moods endlessly fluctuated. While she was candid, even whimsical, about her eating disorder, bulimia nervosa, and her half-hearted suicide attempts, she was at her lowest ebb when speaking about her days inside the royal family, 'the dark ages', as she referred to them. Time and again she emphasized her profound sense of destiny, a belief that she would never become Queen, as well as her awareness that she had been singled out for a special role. She knew in her heart that it was her fate to travel a road where the monarchy was secondary to her true vocation. With hindsight her words have a remarkable prescience.

At times she was amusingly animated, particularly when talking about her short life as a bachelor girl. She spoke wistfully about her romance with Prince Charles, sadly about her unhappy childhood and with some passion about the effect Camilla Parker-Bowles had had on her life. Indeed, she was so anxious not to be seen as paranoid or foolish, as she had been so often told by her husband's friends, that she showed us several letters and postcards from Mrs Parker-Bowles to Prince Charles to prove she was not imagining their relationship.

These billets-doux, passionate, loving and full of suppressed longing, left my publisher and I in absolutely no doubt that Diana's suspicions were correct. Nevertheless, as we were informed by a leading libel lawyer, under stringent British law, the fact that you know something to be true does not allow you to say it. Much to Diana's annoyance and in spite of overwhelming evidence, I was never able to write that Prince Charles and Camilla Parker-Bowles were lovers. Instead I had to allude to a 'secret friendship' which had cast a long shadow over the royal marriage.

I used the opportunity of later interview sessions to fill in many of the gaps which were inevitably left by the first bruisingly honest and virtually seamless narrative of her life story. It took some weeks to appreciate just how powerful was her desire to speak out and, with hindsight, some of my questions were so obviously out of step with the reality of her life that it was inevitable that some of her answers were monosyllabic or simply uncomprehending. Indeed, many events I referred to in my later questions, which the media had deemed significant, had little actual relevance to her life. It meant that the whole interviewing process was very much a hit-and-miss process, trawling through existing material in the hope of hitting on a subject which might spark a response and generate a fresh insight.

Just as the questioning was haphazard, so was the process of gathering the information. I was often told, at very short notice, that Diana had a window of opportunity to answer questions. I would then quickly work out a series of queries relating to her life, pass them on and hope for the best. If her mood was engaged and interested and the questions relevant, then her answers were revealing and penetrating. None the less it was a draining process for her, the taped sessions rarely lasting much more than an hour at any one time. After that the tape recorder was switched off, sometimes prematurely if a member of staff was lurking, and the conversation continued with only a discreetly placed notepad present to jot down relevant material.

As I was working at one remove, I had to second-guess her moods and act accordingly. As a rule of thumb, mornings were times when she was at her most articulate and energetic, particularly if Prince Charles was absent. Those interview sessions were the most productive, Diana speaking with a breathless haste as she poured out her story. She could be unnervingly blithe even when talking about the most intimate and difficult periods of her life. When she first talked about her suicide attempts I naturally needed to know a great deal about when and where they had occurred. I subsequently submitted a raft of specific questions on the subject. When they were presented to her, she treated it as a bit of a joke. 'He's pretty well written my obituary,' she said to her interlocutor.

On the other hand, if a session was arranged for the afternoon, when her energy was low, her conversation was less fruitful. This was particularly so if she had had a bad press or a disagreement with her husband. Then it was usually sensible to focus on happy times, her memories of her bachelor days or her two children, Princes William and Harry. In spite of all these handicaps it was clear as the weeks passed that her excitement and involvement with the project grew, particularly when a title for the book was decided upon. For example, if she knew I was interviewing a trusted friend she would pass on a scrap of information, an anecdote or correction relating to questions I had submitted earlier.

While she was desperate, almost to the point of imprudence, to see her words appear before a wider public, this mood was tempered by a fear that Buckingham Palace would discover her identity as the 'Deep Throat' of my book. As the publishing date approached, the tension at Kensington Palace became palpable. Her newly appointed private secretary, Patrick Jephson described the atmosphere as 'like watching a slowly spreading pool of blood seeping from under a locked door'. In January 1992 she was warned that Buckingham Palace was aware of her co-operation with the book, even though at that stage they did not know its contents. None the less she remained steadfast in co-operating with the venture. The tension was not entirely one-sided; I had been warned on two separate occasions by Fleet Street colleagues that Buckingham Palace was looking hard for my mole. Shortly after one such warning, my offices were burgled and files rifled but nothing of consequence, apart from a camera, was stolen. From then on a scrambler telephone and local pay phones were the only sure way of speaking to her confidants without the worry that the conversations were being bugged.

This problem, however, had been anticipated fairly early on. From the first there was a need to give Diana deniability, developing various ploys so that when she was taken in for interrogation by the Palace guards she could categorically disavow any involvement with the book. The first line of defence were her friends, who were used as cover to disguise her participation. So in tandem with writing questions for the Princess, I sent out a number of begging letters to her circle of friends. They in turn contacted Diana to ask if they should or should not co-operate. It was a patchy process. With some she was encouraging, with others ambivalent, depending on how well she knew them and how close they were to the true nature of the project. Many of those intimately involved truly believed that life couldn't get any worse for Diana, arguing that anything was better than her situation at the time. Inevitably, there was a sense that the dam was about to burst at any moment. Diana's friends spoke with frankness and honesty, bravely aware that their actions would bring the media spotlight upon them. As the Princess herself explained during her television interview: 'A lot of people saw the distress that my life was in, and they felt it was a supportive thing to help in the way that they did.' Her friend and astrologer, Debbie Frank confirmed this mood when she spoke about Diana's life in the months before the book's publication. 'There were times when I would leave a meeting with Diana feeling anxious and concerned because I knew her way was blocked. When Andrew Morton's book was published I was relieved because the world was let into her secret.'

As my interviews progressed, her friends and other acquaintances confirmed that behind the public smiles and glamorous image was a lonely and unhappy young woman who endured a loveless marriage, was seen as an outsider by the Queen and the rest of the royal family and was frequently at odds with the aims and objectives of the royal system. Yet one of the heartening aspects of the story was how Diana was striving, with mixed success, to come to terms with her life; a transformation from a victim to a woman in control of her destiny. It was a process which the Princess continued until the very end.

As the project gained momentum, the acid test came when the Princess read the manuscript. It was delivered to her piecemeal at any and every opportunity. Late one Saturday morning, for example, I cycled to the Brazilian Embassy in Mayfair where the Princess was having lunch with the Ambassador's wife, Lucia Flecha de Lima so that I could pass on the latest offering. Having been given the opportunity to write the story of the best-loved woman in the world I was obviously anxious to know that I had fairly and accurately interpreted her sentiments and her words. To my great relief she read with approval her own words from the taped interviews which were liberally sprinkled throughout the text, either through direct quotation or in the third person. On one occasion Diana was so moved by the poignancy of her own story that she confessed to weeping tears of sorrow. She made a number of alterations, of fact and emphasis, but only one of any significance, a change which gives an insight into her respect for the Queen. During the interviews she said that when she threw herself down the stairs at Sandringham while pregnant with Prince William, the Queen was the first on the scene. On the manuscript, Diana altered the text and inserted the Queen Mother's name, presumably out of deference to the Sovereign.

Even though a number of Diana's close friends were prepared to go on the record in order to underpin the authenticity of the text, the Princess accepted that the book needed a direct link with her own family in order to give it a necessary legitimacy. As a result she agreed to supply the Spencer family albums, containing endless delightful portraits of the growing Diana, many taken by her late father, Earl Spencer. One day several large, red, gold-embossed family albums made their way to the offices of my publisher, Michael O'Mara in South London. A number of photographs were selected, duplicated and the albums returned. The Princess herself helped to identify many of the people who appeared in the photographs with her, a process she greatly enjoyed as it brought back many happy memories, particularly of her teenage years.

She appreciated, too, the fact that, in order to make the book truly distinctive, we had to have a hitherto unpublished jacket picture. As it was out of the question that she could attend a photo shoot, she herself chose and supplied the winsome Patrick Demarchelier cover photograph, which was one she kept in her study at Kensington Palace. This shot, and those of her and her children which were used inside, were her particular favourites.

When the book was published on 16 June 1992 she was relieved that at last her account was out, but desperately anxious that her cover story would hold water. She had to be able to deny involvement when she was put in the dock by the Palace. It was a part she played with aplomb. The author and TV star Clive James fondly recalled asking her over lunch whether she was behind the book. He wrote: 'At least once, however, she lied to me outright. "I really had nothing to do with that Andrew Morton book," she said. "But after my friends talked to him I had to stand by them." She looked me straight

Diana enjoyed herself enormously not least because it brought her sister down a peg or two. Yet it never entered her head for a moment to think that Prince Charles was remotely interested in romance. Certainly she never considered herself a match for the actress Susan George, who was his escort that evening. In any case life was much too fun to think about steady boyfriends. She had returned from her ill starred excursion to a Swiss finishing school desperate to begin an independent life in London. Her parents were not as enthusiastic. Her father, unhappy that she had left West Heath before completing the extra year, was disappointed when she dropped out of her finishing school as well. Not true did!

She had no paper qualifications, no special skills and no burning ambitions bar a vague notion that she wanted to work with children. While Diana seemed destined for a life of unskilled, low paying jobs she was not that much out of the ordinary for girls of her class and background. Aristocratic families traditionally invest more thought and effort in educating boys than girls.

As her father began his fight back to health, Diana's mother took a hand in guiding her career. She wrote to Miss Betty Vacani, the legendary dance teacher who has taught three generations of royal children, and asked if there was a vacancy for a student teacher. There was. Diana passed her interview and, in the spring term, began at the Vacani dance studio on the Brompton Road. It was not a particularly demanding job, basically playing Ring a Ring o' Roses with a group of two-year-olds, but it did combine her love of children with her enjoyment of dance. Again she only lasted three months. For once it wasn't her fault. Ballet teacher course too.

In March her friend Mary-Anne Stewart-Richardson invited her to join her family on their skiing holiday in the French Alps. She fell badly on the slopes, tearing all the tendons in her right ankle. For three months she was in and out of plaster as the tendons slowly heeled. It marked the end of her aspirations as a dance teacher.

What made it worse was that Prince Charles seemed less concerned about her predicament than that of his friend Camilla Parker-Bowles. When he called Diana on the phone he often spoke in sympathetic tones about the rough time Camilla was enjoying because there were three or four press outside her then home of Bolehyde Manor in Wiltshire. Diana bit her lip and said nothing, never mentioning the virtual seige she was living under. She didn't think that it was her place to do so nor did she want to appear to be a burden to the man she ~~longed to marry~~. was in love with

As the romance gathered momentum, Diana began to harbour doubts about her new friend Camilla Parker-Bowles. She seemed to know everything that she and Charles had discussed in their rare moments of privacy and was full of advice on how best to handle Prince Charles. It was all very strange. Even Diana, an absolute

Diana made a number of alterations to the original manuscript in her own hand.

in the eye when she said this, so I could see how plausible she could be when she was telling a whopper.'

As a result of the necessary distance she put between herself and the book it meant that I, her friends and others were effectively fighting her corner with one hand behind our backs. In the face of the barrage of abuse and vilification which greeted the book's three central assertions, namely Diana's eating disorder, bulimia nervosa, her suicide attempts and Prince Charles's relationship with Camilla Parker-Bowles, it is an understatement to say that it would have been helpful if she had announced her complete co-operation. Indeed, the animosity, scepticism and sheer vitriol with which the Establishment and their media acolytes first greeted the publication of my book graphically demonstrated the difficulties of presenting the truth to the British public.

In the months following that momentous event, the book not only altered the way the public viewed the monarchy and forced the Prince and Princess of Wales finally to address the ruins of their marriage, it also brought the one thing Diana had dreamed of – hope; the chance of fulfilment, of freedom and of a future where she was liberated at last to be a person in her own right. In the past five years, particularly the last few months of her life, the world witnessed the flowering of Diana's true nature, qualities which would have remained buried if she had not had the courage and determination to tell her public about the reality of her life. Diana achieved that aim, and the public's verdict can be gauged by the mountain of flowers outside Kensington Palace and elsewhere and the outpouring of grief that has convulsed not just her own country but the rest of the world.

While the public's image of Diana underwent an astonishing transformation when her story was told, I don't think she ever truly thought through the consequences of her actions. As she said on television when asked that question: 'I don't know. Maybe people have a better understanding, maybe there's a lot of women out there who suffer on the same level but in a different environment who are unable to stand up for themselves because their self-esteem is cut in two.' Once again her instinct about the response was unerring as literally thousands of women, many from America, expressed how, through reading about her life, they had discovered and explored something in their own lives. Her motivation was first and foremost a desperate cry for help, an appeal over the heads of the Palace who confined her, to the people who loved her. She wanted to make known to those people her *true story*, so that they might judge her worth for themselves.

She may now be gone, but her words are with us for ever. When I wrote *Diana, Her True Story* her testimony was used *sotto voce* throughout the text – in short, direct quotation or through third parties. One of the abiding sadnesses of her short life was that she never truly had the chance to 'sing openly'. If she had enjoyed a full life she would probably have written her own memoirs at some point. Sadly, that is no longer possible. The testimony which follows is her life story as she wanted to tell it. Her words are now all we have of her, her testament, the nearest we will now ever get to her autobiography. No-one can deny her that.

Diana, Princess of Wales
In Her Own Words

Publisher's note: The following words are selected from those given by Diana, Princess of Wales in 1991–2 to Andrew Morton for publication in Diana, Her True Story. *The words are all Diana's except for those in parentheses.*

Childhood

[My first memory] is really the smell of the inside of my pram. It was plastic and the smell of the hood. Vivid memory. I was born at home not in hospital.

The biggest disruption was when Mummy decided to leg it. That's the vivid memory we have – the four of us. We all have our own interpretations of what should have happened and what did happen. People took sides. Various people didn't speak to each other. For my brother and I it was a very wishy-washy and painful experience.

Charles [her brother] said to me the other day that he hadn't realized how much the divorce had affected him until he got married and started having a life of his own. But my other sisters – their growing up was done out of my sight. I saw them at holidays. I don't remember it being a big thing.

I idolized my eldest sister and I used to do all her washing when she came back from school. I packed her suitcase, ran her bath, made her bed – the whole lot. I did it all and I thought it was wonderful. I always looked after my brother really. My sisters were very independent.

We had so many changes of nannies. My brother and I, if we didn't like them we used to stick pins in their chair and throw their clothes out of the window. We always thought they were a threat because they tried to take mother's position. They were all rather young and pretty. They were chosen by my father. It was terribly disruptive to come back from school one day to find a new nanny.

I always felt very different from everyone else, very detached. I knew I was going somewhere different but had no idea where. I said to my father when I was aged 13, 'I know I'm going to marry someone in the public eye,' thinking more of being an ambassador's wife – not the top one, very much so. It was a very unhappy childhood. Parents were busy sorting themselves out. Always seeing my mother crying. Daddy never spoke to us about it. We never asked questions. Too many changes over nannies, very unstable, the whole thing. Generally unhappy and being very detached from everybody else.

At the age of 14 I just remember thinking that I wasn't very good at anything, that I was hopeless. My brother was always the one getting exams at school and I was the dropout. I couldn't understand why I was perhaps a nuisance to have around which, in later years, I've perceived as being part of the [whole question of the] son, the child who died before me was a son and both [parents] were crazy to have a son and heir and there comes a third daughter. What a bore, we're going to have to try again. I've recognized that now. I've been aware of it and now I recognize it and that's fine. I accept it.

I adored animals, guinea pigs and all that. In my bed I'd have 20 stuffed bed animals and there would be a midget's space for me, and they would have to be in my bed every night. That was my family. I hated the dark and had an obsession about the dark, always had to have a light outside my door until I was at least ten. I used to hear my brother crying in his bed down at the other end of the house, crying for my mother and he was unhappy too, and my father right down the other end of the house and it was always very difficult. I never could pluck up courage to get out of bed. I remember it to this day.

I remember Mummy crying an awful lot and every Saturday when we went up for weekends, every Saturday night, standard procedure, she would start crying. On Saturday we would both see her crying. 'What's the matter, Mummy?' 'Oh, I don't want you to leave tomorrow,' which for a nine-year-old was devastating, you know. I remember the most agonizing decision I ever had to make. I was a bridesmaid to my first cousin and to go to the rehearsal I had to be smart and wear a dress and my mother gave me a green dress and my father had given me a white dress and they were both so smart, the dresses, and I can't remember to this day which one I got in but I remember being totally traumatized by it because it would show favouritism.

I remember there being a great discussion that a judge was going to come to me at Riddlesworth [Diana's preparatory school] and say who would I prefer to live with. The judge never turned up and then suddenly my stepfather [Peter Shand Kydd] arrived on the scene. Charles and I, my brother and I, went up to London and I said to Mummy, 'Where is he? Where is your new husband?' 'He's at the ticket barrier,' and there was this very good-looking, handsome man and we were longing to love him and we accepted him and he was great to us, spoilt us rotten. It was very nice being spoilt because [my] individual parents weren't attuned to that. Basically, we couldn't wait to be independent, Charles and I, in order to spread our wings and do our own thing. We had become horribly different at school because we had divorced parents and nobody else did at that time, but by the time we finished our five years at prep school everybody was. I was always different. I always had this thing inside me that I was different. I didn't know why. I couldn't even talk about it but in my mind it was there.

The divorce helped me to relate to anyone else who is upset in their family life, whether it be stepfather syndrome or mother or whatever, I understand it. Been there, done it.

I always got on very well with everybody. Whether it be the gardener, or the local police or whoever, I went over to talk to them. My father always said: 'Treat everybody as an individual and never throw your weight around.'

My father used to sit us down every Christmas and birthday and we had to write our thank-you letters within 24 hours.

And now if I don't, I get into a panic. If I come back from a dinner party or somewhere that needs a letter, at midnight I'll sit down and write it there and not wait until next morning because it would wrestle with my conscience. And William now does it – it's great. It's nice if other people appreciate it at the other end.

We were all shunted over to Sandringham [the Queen's Norfolk residence] for holidays. Used to go and see *Chitty Chitty Bang Bang*, the film. We hated it so much. We hated going over there. The atmosphere was always very strange when we went there and I used to kick and fight anyone who tried to make us go over there and Daddy was most insistent because it was rude. I said I didn't want to see *Chitty Chitty Bang Bang* for the third year running. Holidays were always very grim because we had a four-week holiday. Two weeks Mummy and two weeks Daddy and the trauma of going from one house to another and each individual parent trying to make it up in their area with material things rather than the actual tactile stuff, which is what we both craved for but neither of us ever got. When I say neither of us my other two sisters were busy at prep school and were sort of out of the house whereas my brother and I were very much stuck together.

Schooldays

Adored that [her preparatory school, Riddlesworth Hall]. I felt rejected, though, because I was busy looking after my father most of the time and then suddenly realized I was going to be away from him so I used to make threats like, 'if you love me you won't leave me here,' which was jolly unkind to him at the time. Actually, I loved being at school. I was very naughty in the sense of always wanting to laugh and muck about rather than sit tight looking at the four walls of the schoolroom.

[I remember school plays] and the thrill of putting on make-up. It was one of those nativity plays. I was one of the twits who came and paid homage to the baby Jesus. In another I was a Dutch doll. But I never put myself forward to speak in a play. I never read the lessons at school. I would go quietly. When

I was asked to act I would only do it on the condition that I didn't have to speak.

[My first sporting cup] was diving. I won it four years running if you are going to be honest! I always won all the swimming and diving cups. I won all sorts of prizes for the best-kept guinea pig. But in the academic department, you might as well forget about that! [Laughter.]

At school we were only allowed one animal on the bed. I had a green hippo and painted his eyes luminous so that at night – I hated the dark – it looked as though he was looking at me!

I nearly got expelled because one night somebody said to me: 'Would I like to do a dare?' I thought 'Why not? Life's so boring.' So they sent me out at 9 o'clock to the end of the drive which was half a mile long in pitch dark. I had to go and get some sweets at the gate from somebody called Polly Phillimore. I got there and there was nobody there.

I hid behind the gate as these police cars were coming in. I thought nothing more about it. I saw all the lights coming on in the school. I thought nothing about it. I wandered back, terrified, to find that some twit in my bedroom said that she had appendicitis. Then they asked 'Where's Diana?' 'Don't know.'

Both parents, then divorced, were summoned. Father was thrilled and my mother said: 'I didn't think you had it in you.' No telling off.

I ate and ate and ate. It was always a great joke – let's get Diana to have three kippers at breakfast and six pieces of bread, and I did all that.

My sister [Jane] was a prefect at West Heath School, and I was pretty ghastly for the first term. I was a bully because I thought it was so wonderful to have my sister as a prefect. I felt very important but the second term they all paid me back, all the people I was horrid to and by the third term I was completely calm and sorted out.

There was an enormous hall there which they had just built on. I used to sneak down at night when it was all dark and put on my music and do my ballet there in this enormous hall for hours on end and no-one ever found me. All my friends knew where I was when I crept out and it always released tremendous tension in my head. I recognize it now but at the time it just seemed a good idea.

I liked all subjects. I played the piano. I loved the piano. I did my tap dancing which I absolutely adored, tennis, I was captain of the netball team, hockey, you name it because of my height. I was one of the tallest there. I adored being outdoors again, visited old people once a week, went to the local mental asylum once a week. I adored that. It was a sort of introduction for bigger things. Then, by the time I got to the top of the school, all my friends had boyfriends but not me because I knew somehow that I had to keep myself very tidy for whatever was coming my way.

I wasn't a good child in the sense that I had horns in my ears. I was always looking for trouble. Yes, I was popular. I didn't shout out the answers in class because I didn't think I knew them. But I always knew how to behave. There was a time to be quiet and a time to be noisy. I could always tune in to which it should be.

I had crushes, serious crushes on all sorts of people, especially my sisters' boyfriends. If they ever got chucked out from that department I used to try my way. I felt so sorry for them because they were so nice. That was purely it. Anyway, that was a dead miss.

Moving to Althorp

When I was 13 we moved to Althorp in Northampton and that was a terrible wrench, leaving Norfolk, because that's where everybody who I'd grown up with lived. We had to move because grandfather died and life took a very big turn because my stepmother, Raine, appeared on the scene, supposedly incognito. She used to sort of join us, accidentally find us in places and come and sit down and pour us with presents and we all hated her so much because we thought she was going to take Daddy away from us but actually she was suffering from the same thing.

She wanted to marry Daddy, that was her target and that was it. I've sat and boiled for years and years and two Septembers ago [1989] my brother got married and I told her what I thought about her and I've never known such anger in me. I took it upon myself to air everyone's grievances in my family. I stuck up for Mummy and my mother said that was the first time in 22 years anyone had ever stuck up for her. I said everything I possibly could. I remember really going for her gullet – I was so angry. I said: 'I hate you so much, if only you knew how much we all hated you for what you've done, you've ruined the house, you spend Daddy's money and what for?'

Diana's father's illness

And he had a haemorrhage, a brain haemorrhage. He suffered headaches, took Disprins, told nobody. I had a premonition that he was going to be ill whilst I was staying with some friends in Norfolk and they said: 'How's your father?' and I said: 'I've got this strange feeling that he's going to drop down and if he dies, he'll die immediately otherwise he'll survive.' I heard myself say this – thought nothing more about it. Next day the telephone rang and I said to the lady, that will be about Daddy. It was. He'd collapsed. I was frightfully calm, went back up to London, went to the hospital, saw Daddy was gravely ill. They said: 'He's going to die.' The brain had ruptured and we saw another side of Raine which we hadn't anticipated as she basically blocked us out of the hospital, she wouldn't let us see Daddy. My eldest sister took charge of that and went in sometimes to see him. Meanwhile, he couldn't talk because he had a tracheotomy so he wasn't able to ask where his other children were. Goodness knows what he was thinking because no-one was telling him. Anyway, he got better and he basically changed character. He was one person before and he was certainly a different person after. He's remained estranged but adoring since.

On her brother

I've always seen him as the brains in the family. I still see that. He's got S-levels and things like that. I think that my brother, being the youngest and the only boy, was quite precious because Althorp is a big place. Remember I was the girl who was supposed to be a boy. Being third in line was a very good position to be in – I got away with murder. I was my father's favourite, there's no doubt about that.

I longed to be as good as Charles in the schoolroom. I was never jealous of him. I so understand him. He's very like me as opposed to my two sisters. Like me he will always suffer. There's something in us that attracts that department. Whereas my two sisters are blissfully happy being detached from various situations.

I know that when I went to finishing school [the Institut Alpin Videmanette in Switzerland] I wrote something like 120 letters in the first month. I was so unhappy there – I just wrote and wrote and wrote. I felt out of place there. I learned how to ski but I wasn't very good with everybody else. It was just too claustrophobic for me albeit it was in the mountains. I did one term there. When I found out how much it cost to send me there I told them it was a waste of their money. They whipped me back.

My parents said: 'You can't come to London until you are 18, you can't have a flat until you are 18.' So I went and worked with a family in Headley Borden in Hampshire, Philippa and Jeremy Whitaker. I looked after their one daughter, Alexandra, and lived as part of their team. It was all right. I was itching to go to London because I thought the grass was greener on the other side.

Bachelor girl in London

It was nice being in a flat with the girls. I loved that – it was great. I laughed my head off there. I kept myself to myself. I wasn't interested in having a full diary. I loved being on my own, as I do now – a great treat.

[On her nannying jobs] They were often pretty grim employers – velvet hairbands. I was sent out to all sorts of people from my sisters – their friends were producing rapidly. They sent me out the whole time – bliss. Solve Your Problems [employment agency] sent me on cleaning missions which I liked but nobody ever thanked me for it.

I did a cookery course in Wimbledon. I quite liked it, but more velvet hairbands. I got terribly fat. I loved sauces, my fingers were always in the saucepans for which I got fined. It wasn't my idea of fun but my parents wanted me to do it. At the time it seemed a better alternative than being behind a typewriter – and I got a diploma!

Meeting the Prince of Wales

I've known her [the Queen] since I was tiny so it was no big deal. No interest in Andrew and Edward – never thought about Andrew. I kept thinking, 'Look at the life they have, how awful' so I remember him coming to Althorp to stay, my husband, and the first impact was 'God, what a sad man.' He came with his labrador. My sister was all over him like a bad rash and I thought, 'God, he must really hate that.' I kept out of the way. I remember being a fat, podgy, no make-up, unsmart lady but I made a lot of noise and he liked that and he came up to me after dinner and we had a big dance and he said: 'Will you show me the gallery?' and I was just about to show him the gallery and my sister Sarah comes up and tells me to push off and I said 'At least, let me tell you where the switches are to the gallery because you won't know where they are,' and I disappeared. And he was charm himself and when I stood next to him the next day, a 16-year old, for someone like that to show you any attention – I was just so sort of amazed. 'Why would anyone like him be interested in me?' and it *was* interest. That was it for about two years. Saw him off and on with Sarah and Sarah got frightfully excited about the whole thing, then she saw something different happening which I hadn't twigged on to, i.e. when he had his 30th birthday dance I was asked too.

'Why is Diana coming as well?' [my] sister asked. I said: 'Well, I don't know but I'd like to come.' 'Oh, all right then,' that sort of thing. Had a very nice time at the dance – fascinating. I wasn't at all intimidated by the surroundings [Buckingham Palace]. I thought, amazing place.

Then I was asked to stay at the de Passes in July 1980 by Philip de Pass who is the son. 'Would you like to come and stay for a couple of nights down at Petworth because we've got the Prince of Wales staying. You're a young blood, you might amuse him.' So I said 'OK.' So I sat next to him and Charles came in. He was all over me again and it was very strange. I thought 'Well, this isn't very cool.' I thought men were supposed not to be so obvious, I thought this was very odd. The first night we sat down on a bale at the barbecue at this house and he'd just finished with Anna Wallace. I said: 'You looked so sad when you walked up the aisle at Lord Mountbatten's funeral.' I said: 'It was the most tragic thing I've ever seen. My heart bled for you when I watched. I thought, "It's wrong, you're lonely – you should be with somebody to look after you."'

The next minute he leapt on me practically and I thought this was very strange, too, and I wasn't quite sure how to cope with all this. Anyway we talked about lots of things and anyway that was it. Frigid wasn't the word. Big F when it comes to that. He said: 'You must come to London with me tomorrow. I've got to work at Buckingham Palace, you must come to work with me.' I thought this was too much. I said: 'No, I can't.' I thought 'How will I explain my presence at Buckingham Palace when I'm supposed to be staying with Philip?' Then he asked me to Cowes on *Britannia* and he had lots of older friends there and I was fairly intimidated but they were all over me like a bad rash. I felt very strange about the whole thing, obviously somebody was talking.

I came in and out, in and out, then I went to stay with my sister Jane at Balmoral where Robert [Fellowes, Jane's husband] was assistant private secretary [to the Queen]. I was terrified – shitting bricks. I was frightened because I had never stayed at Balmoral and I wanted to get it right. The anticipation was worse than actually being there. I was all right once I got in through the front door. I had a normal single bed! I have always done my own packing and unpacking – I was always appalled that Prince Charles takes 22 pieces of hand luggage with him. That's before the other stuff. I have four or five. I felt rather embarrassed.

I stayed back at the castle because of the press interest. It was considered a good idea. Mr and Mrs Parker-Bowles were there at all my visits. I was the youngest there by a long way. Charles used to ring me up and say: 'Would you like to come for a walk, come for a barbecue?' so I said: 'Yes, please.' I thought this was all wonderful.

Courtship

Then it sort of built up from there, then the press seized upon it. Then that became simply unbearable in our flat but my three girls were wonderful, star performers; loyalty beyond belief. The feeling was I wish Prince Charles would hurry up and get on with it. The Queen was fed up. Then Charles rang me up from Klosters and said: 'I've got something to ask you.' Instinct in a female, you know what's coming. Anyway, I sat up all night with my girls, saying 'What do I say, what do I do?' bearing in mind that there's somebody else around.

By that time I'd realized there was somebody else around. I'd been staying at Bolehyde with the Parker-Bowleses an awful lot and I couldn't understand why she [Camilla] kept saying to me, 'Don't push him into doing this, don't do that.' She knew so much about what he was doing privately and about what we were doing privately . . . if we were going to stay at Broadlands, I couldn't understand it. Eventually I worked it all out and found the proof of the pudding and people were willing to talk to me.

Anyway, next day I went to Windsor and I arrived about 5 o'clock and he sat me down and said: 'I've missed you so much.' But there was never anything tactile about him. It was extraordinary, but I didn't have anything to go by because I had never had a boyfriend. I'd always kept them away, thought they were all trouble – and I couldn't handle it emotionally, I was very screwed up, I thought. Anyway, so he said 'Will you marry me?' and I laughed. I remember thinking, 'This is a joke,' and I said: 'Yeah, OK,' and laughed. He was deadly serious. He said: 'You do realize that one day you will be Queen.' And a voice said to me inside: 'You won't be Queen but you'll have a tough role.' So I thought 'OK,' so I said: 'Yes.' I said: 'I love you so much, I love you so much.' He said: 'Whatever love means.' He said it then. So I thought that was great! I thought he meant that! And so he ran upstairs and rang his mother.

In my immaturity, which was enormous, I thought that he was very much in love with me, which he was, but he always had a sort of besotted look about him, looking back at it, but it wasn't the genuine sort. 'Who was this girl who was so different?' but he couldn't understand it because his immaturity was quite big in that department too. For me it was like a call of duty, really – to go and work with the people.

I came back to the flat and sat on my bed. 'Guess what?' They said: 'He asked you. What did you say?' 'Yes please.' Everybody screamed and howled and we went for a drive around London with our secret. I rang my parents the next morning. Daddy was thrilled. 'How wonderful.' Mummy was thrilled. I told my brother and he said 'Who to?'

I then went away two days later to Australia for three weeks to sort of settle down and to organize lists and things with my mother. That was a complete disaster because I pined for him but he never rang me up. I thought that was very strange and whenever I rang him he was out and he never rang me back. I thought 'OK.' I was just being generous – 'He is being very busy, this, that and the other.' I come back from Australia, someone knocks on my door – someone from his office with a bunch of flowers and I knew that they hadn't come from Charles because there was no note. It was just somebody being very tactful in the office.

Press harassment

Then it all started to build up, sort of like the press were being unbearable following my every move. I understood they had a job, but people did not understand they had binoculars on me the whole time. They hired the opposite flat in Old Brompton Road, which was a library which looked into my bedroom, and it wasn't fair on the girls. I couldn't put the telephone off the hook in case any of their family were ill in the night. The papers used to ring me up at 2am – they were just putting out another story – 'Could I confirm it or deny it?'

I failed once [her driving test] and then got it second time. With the media I always made sure that I was going through the lights just as the light was turning red, so they were stuck. When I got into my car, they'd chase me everywhere. You're talking about 30 of them – not two.

I had to get out of Coleherne Court once to go to stay with him [Prince Charles] at Broadlands. So we took my sheets off the bed and I got out of the kitchen window, which is on the side street, with a suitcase. I did it that way round.

I was constantly polite, constantly civil. I was never rude. I never shouted. I cried like a baby to the four walls. I just couldn't cope with it. I cried because I got no support from Charles and no support from the Palace press office. They just said: 'You're on your own' so I thought 'Fine.'

[Prince Charles] wasn't at all supportive. Whenever he rang me up he said: 'Poor Camilla Parker-Bowles. I've had her on the telephone tonight and she says there's lots of press at Bolehyde. She's having a very rough time.' I never complained about the press to him because I didn't think it was my position to do so. I asked him: 'How many press are out there?' He said 'At least four.' I thought 'My God, there's 34 here!' and I never told him.

I was able to recognize an inner determination to survive. Anyway, thank God, it got announced [the engagement] and before I knew what happened, I was in Clarence House [the London residence of the Queen Mother]. Nobody there to welcome me. It was like going into a hotel. Then everyone said: 'Why are you at Clarence House?' and I said I was told that I was expected to be at Clarence House. And I'd left my flat for the last time and suddenly I had a policeman. And my policeman the night before the engagement said to me: 'I just want you to know that this is your last night of freedom ever in the rest of your life, so make the most of it.' It was like a sword went in my heart. I thought 'God,' then I sort of giggled like an immature girl.

It was about three days before we went to the Palace [from Clarence House]. At Clarence House I remember being woken in the morning by a very sweet elderly lady who brought in all the papers about the engagement and put them on my bed.

Marrying into the royal family

My grandma [Ruth, Lady Fermoy] always said to me: 'Darling, you must understand that their sense of humour and their lifestyle are different and I don't think it will suit you.'

The attractions of becoming a princess

You see, I had a very good lifestyle myself. I had my own money and lived in a big house. So it wasn't as though I was going into anything different.

Choosing the engagement ring

A briefcase comes along on the pretext that Andrew is getting a signet ring for his 21st birthday and along come these sapphires. I mean *nuggets*! I suppose I chose it, we all chipped in. The Queen paid for it.

That black dress

I remember my first [royal] engagement so well. *So* excited. Black dress from the Emanuels and I thought it was OK because girls my age wore this dress. I hadn't appreciated that I was now seen as a royal lady, although I'd only got a ring on my finger as opposed to two rings.

Black to me was the smartest colour you could possibly have at the age of 19. It was a real grown-up dress. I was quite big-chested then and they all got frightfully excited. I remember meeting Princess Grace and how wonderful and serene she was but there was troubled water under her, I saw that.

It was a horrendous occasion. I didn't know whether to go out of the door first. I didn't know whether your handbag should be in your left hand not your right hand. I was terrified really – at the time everything was all over the place.

Engagement

I missed my girls so much I wanted to go back there and sit and giggle like we used to and borrow clothes and chat about silly things, just being in my safe shell again. One day you've got the King and Queen of Sweden coming to give you their wedding present of four brass candlesticks, the next minute you get the President of Somewhere Else coming to see. I was just pushed into the fire but I have to say my upbringing was able to handle that. It wasn't as though I was picked out like *My Fair Lady* and told to get on with it. I did know how to react.

[On impressions of Buckingham Palace] I couldn't believe how cold everyone was. I was told one thing but actually another thing was going on. The lies and the deceit. For example, my husband sending Camilla Parker-Bowles flowers when she had meningitis. 'To Gladys from Fred.'

Meeting Camilla

[I met her] very early on. I was introduced to the circle, but obviously I was a threat. I was a very young girl but I was a threat.

We always had discussions about Camilla though. I once heard him on the telephone in his bath on his hand-held set saying: 'Whatever happens, I will always love you.' I told him afterwards that I had listened at the door and we had a filthy row.

When I arrived at Clarence House there was a letter on my bed from Camilla, dated two days previously, saying 'Such exciting news about the engagement. Do let's have lunch soon when the Prince of Wales goes to Australia and New Zealand. He's going to be away for three weeks. I'd love to see the ring, lots of love, Camilla.' and that was 'Wow!' So I organized lunch. We had lunch and, bearing in mind that I was so immature, I didn't know about jealousy or depressions or anything like that. I had such a wonderful existence being a kindergarten teacher – you didn't suffer from anything like that, you got tired but that was it. There was no-one around to give you grief. So we had lunch. Very tricky indeed. She said: 'You are not going to hunt are you?' I said: 'On what?' She said: 'Horse. You are not going to hunt when you go and live at Highgrove are you?' I said: 'No.' She said: 'I just wanted to know,' and I thought as far as she was concerned that was her communication route. Still too immature to understand all the messages coming my way.

Anyway, somebody in his office told me that my husband had had a bracelet made for her which she wears to this day. It's a gold chain bracelet with a blue enamel disc. It's got 'G and F' entwined in it, 'Gladys' and 'Fred' – they were their nicknames. I walked into this man's office one day and said: 'Oh, what's in that parcel?' He said: 'Oh, you shouldn't look at that.' I said: 'Well, I'm going to look at it.' I opened it and there was a bracelet and I said: 'I know where this is going.' I was devastated. This was about two weeks before we got married. He said: 'Well, he's going to give it to her tonight.' So rage, rage, rage! 'Why can't you be honest with me?' But, no, he [Prince Charles] cut me absolutely dead. It's as if he had made his decision, and if it wasn't going to work, it wasn't going to work. He'd found the virgin, the sacrificial lamb, and in a way he was obsessed with me. But it was hot and cold, hot and cold. You never knew what mood it was going to be, up and down, up and down.

He took the bracelet, lunchtime on Monday, we got married on the Wednesday. I went to his policeman who was back in the office and said: 'John, where's Prince Charles?' and he said: 'Oh, he's gone out for lunch.' So I said: 'Why are you here? Shouldn't you be with him?' 'Oh, I'm going to collect him later.'

So I went upstairs, had lunch with my sisters who were there and said: 'I can't marry him, I can't do this, this is absolutely unbelievable.' They were wonderful and said: 'Well, bad luck, Duch, your face is on the tea-towels so you're too late to chicken out.' So we made light of it.

I never dealt with that side of things. I just said to him: 'You must always be honest with me.' On our honeymoon, for instance, we were opening our diaries to discuss various things. Out comes two pictures of Camilla. On our honeymoon we have our white tie dinner for President Sadat [of Egypt]. Cufflinks arrive on his wrists – two 'C's entwined like the Chanel 'C's. Got it in one; knew exactly. 'Camilla gave you those didn't she?' He said: 'Yes, so what's wrong? They're a present from a friend.' And, boy, did we have a row. Jealousy, total jealousy – and it's such a good idea the two 'C's but it wasn't that clever in some ways.

I was the only one here [when planning the wedding] because he had pushed off to Australia and New Zealand on tour, and you may recall, of course, the picture of me sobbing in a red coat when he went off in the aeroplane. It had nothing to do with him going. The most awful thing had happened before he went. I was in his study talking to him, when the telephone rang. It was Camilla, just before he was going for five weeks. I thought, 'Shall I be nice or shall I just sit here?' So I thought I'd be nice so I left them to it. It just broke my heart that.

Highgrove House

He said he wanted to be in the Duchy [of Cornwall] vicinity but it's only 11 miles from her house. He chose the house and I came along afterwards. First went there after he bought it. He had painted all the walls white. He wanted me to do it up even though we were not engaged. I thought it was very improper but he liked my taste.

The Highgrove Set

I started to think, 'Gosh, they talk rather strangely to me.' I was very normal in the sense that I said what I thought because nobody ever told me to shut up. They were all oiling up, basically, kissing his feet and I thought it was so bad for an individual to receive all that.

Decorating two new homes

[Dudley Poplak] did up my mother's house 10 years previously and had always been a friend of my mother's, so I said to her: 'What do you think?' She said: 'Well, use him, he's been marvellous, very loyal.' I chose the decorations and had a free hand to do that.

Choosing St Paul's or Westminster Abbey

Prince Charles said that people could see more and the acoustics were better [at St Paul's]. Great debate in the family about it, it had never happened before. 'I want it that way,' Charles said. Great confusion.

Wedding presents

Charles and I went around the General Trading Company [a fashionable gift store frequented by the Establishment]. Looking back on it was quite a funny thing to do – so Sloane!

The wedding

Great anticipation. Happiness because the crowds buoyed you up – I don't think I was happy. We got married on Wednesday and on the Monday we had gone to St Paul's for our last rehearsal and that's when the camera lights were on full and a sense of what the day was going to be. And I sobbed my eyes out. Absolutely collapsed and it was collapsing because of all sorts of things. The Camilla thing rearing its head the whole way through our engagement and I was desperately trying to be mature about the situation but I didn't have the foundations to do it and I couldn't talk to anyone about it.

I remember my husband being very tired – both of us were quite tired. Big day. He sent me a very nice signet ring the night before to Clarence House, with the Prince of Wales feathers on and a very nice card that said: 'I'm so proud of you and when you come up I'll be there at the altar for you tomorrow. Just look 'em in the eye and knock 'em dead.'

I had a very bad fit of bulimia the night before. I ate everything I could possible find which amused my sister [Jane] because she was staying at Clarence House with me and nobody understood what was going on there. It was very hush-hush. I was sick as a parrot that night. It was such an indication of what was going on.

I was very calm the next morning when we were getting up at Clarence House. Must have been awake about 5am. Interesting – they put me in a bedroom overlooking the Mall which meant I didn't get any sleep. I was very, very calm, deathly calm. I felt I was a lamb to the slaughter. I knew it and couldn't do anything about it. My last night of freedom with Jane at Clarence House.

Father was so thrilled he waved himself stupid. We went past St Martin-in-the-Fields and he thought we were at St Paul's. He was ready to get out. It was wonderful, that.

As I walked up the aisle I was looking for her [Camilla]. I knew she was in there, of course. I looked for her. Anyway I got up to the top. I thought the whole thing was hysterical, getting married, in the sense that it was just like it was so grown up and here was Diana – a kindergarten teacher. The whole thing was ridiculous!

I cried a lot on the Monday when we had done the rehearsal because the tension had suddenly hit me. But by Wednesday I was fine and I had to get my father basically up the aisle and that's what I concentrated on and I remember being terribly worried about curtseying to the Queen. I remember being so in love with my husband that I couldn't take my eyes off him. I just absolutely thought I was the luckiest girl in the world.

He was going to look after me. Well, was I wrong on that assumption.

So walking down the aisle I spotted Camilla, pale grey, veiled pillbox hat, saw it all, her son Tom standing on a chair. To this day you know – vivid memory. Well, there you are, that's it, let's hope that's all over with. Got out [of St Paul's], was a wonderful feeling, everybody hurraying, everybody happy because they thought we were happy and there was the big question mark in my mind. I realized I had taken on an enormous role but had no idea what I was going into – but *no* idea.

Back to Buckingham Palace, did all the photographs, nothing tactile, nothing. I was basically wandering around trying to find where I should be, clutching my long train with my bridesmaids and pages. Got out on the balcony, overwhelming what we saw, so humble-making, all these thousands and thousands of people happy. It was just wonderful. Sat next to him at the wedding breakfast, which was a lunch. Neither of us spoke to each other – we were so shattered. I was exhausted at the whole thing.

Honeymoon

I never tried to call it off in the sense of of really doing that but the worst moment was when we got to Broadlands. I thought, you know, it was just grim. I just had tremendous hope in me, which was slashed by day two. Went to Broadlands. Second night, out come the van der Post novels he hadn't read [Laurens van der Post, the South African philosopher and adventurer, was much admired by Prince Charles]. Seven of them – they came on our honeymoon. He read them and we had to analyse them over lunch every day. We had to entertain the boardroom on *Britannia*, which were all the top people every night so there was never any time on our own. Found that very difficult to accept. By then the bulimia was appalling, absolutely appalling. It was rife, four times a day on the yacht. Anything I could find I would gobble up and be sick two minutes later – very tired. So, of course, that slightly got the mood swings going in the sense that one minute one would be happy, next blubbing one's eyes out.

I remember crying my eyes out on our honeymoon. I was so tired, for all the wrong reasons totally.

Went off to Balmoral straight from the yacht, everyone was there to welcome us and then the realization set in. My dreams were appalling. At night I dreamt of Camilla the whole time. Charles got Laurens van der Post up to come and help me. Laurens didn't understand me. Everybody saw I was getting thinner and thinner and I was being sicker and sicker. Basically they thought I could adapt to being Princess of Wales overnight. Anyway, a godsend, William was conceived in October. Marvellous news, occupied my mind.

Obsessed by Camilla totally. Didn't trust him, thought every five minutes he was ringing her up asking how to handle his marriage. All the guests at Balmoral coming to stay just stared at me the whole time, treated me like glass. As far as I was concerned I was Diana, the only difference was people called me 'Ma'am' now, 'Your Royal Highness', and they curtseyed. That was the only difference, but I treated everybody else exactly the same.

Charles used to want to go for long walks around Balmoral the whole time when we were on our honeymoon. His idea of enjoyment would be to sit on top of the highest hill at Balmoral. It is beautiful up there. I completely understand; he would read Laurens van der Post or Jung to me, and bear in mind I hadn't a clue about psychic powers or anything, but I knew there was something in me that hadn't been awoken yet and I didn't think this was going to help! So anyway we read those and I did my tapestry and he was blissfully happy, and as far as he was happy that was fine.

He was in awe of his Mama, intimidated by his father, and I was always the third person in the room. It was never 'Darling, would you like a drink?' it was always 'Mummy, would you like a drink?' 'Granny, would you like a drink?' 'Diana, would you like a drink?' Fine, no problem. But I had to be told that that was normal because I always thought it was the wife first – stupid thought!

Terribly, terribly thin. People started commenting 'Your bones are showing.' So that was the October and then we stayed up there [at Balmoral] from August to October. By October I was about to cut my wrists. I was in a very bad way. It rained and rained and rained and I came down early from Balmoral to seek treatment, not because I hated Balmoral but because I was in such a bad way. Anyway, came down here [London]. All the analysts and psychiatrists you could ever dream of came plodding in trying to sort me out. Put me on high doses of Valium and everything else. But the Diana that was still very much there had decided it was just time; patience and adapting were all that were needed. It was me telling them what I needed. They were telling me 'pills'! That was going to keep them happy – they could go to bed at night and sleep, knowing the Princess of Wales wasn't going to stab anyone.

Pregnancy

Then I was told I was pregnant, fine, great excitement, then we went to Wales for three days to do our visit as Princess and Prince of Wales. Boy, oh boy, was that a culture shock in every sense of the word. Wrong clothes, wrong everything, wrong timing, feeling terribly sick, carrying this child, hadn't told the world I was pregnant but looking grey and gaunt and still being sick. Desperately trying to make him proud of me. Made a speech in Welsh. He was more nervous than I was. Never got any praise for it. I began to understand that that was absolutely normal. Sick as a parrot, rained the whole time round Wales. It wasn't easy, I cried a lot in the car, saying I couldn't get out, couldn't cope with the crowds. 'Why had they come to see us? Someone help me.' He said: 'You've just got to get out and do it.' I just got out. He tried his hardest and he did really well in that department, got me out and once I was out I was able to do my bit. But it cost me such a lot because I hadn't got the energy because I was being sick with my bulimia – so much; let alone the support for him or vice versa.

Couldn't sleep, didn't eat, whole world was collapsing around me. Very, very difficult pregnancy indeed. Sick the whole time, bulimia *and* morning sickness. People tried to put me on pills to stop me from being sick. I refused. So sick, sick, sick, sick, sick. And this family's never had anybody who's had morning sickness before, so every time at Balmoral, Sandringham or Windsor in my evening dress I had to go out I either fainted or was sick. It was so embarrassing because I didn't know anything because I hadn't read my books but I knew it was morning sickness because you just do. So I was 'a problem' and they registered Diana as 'a problem'. 'She's different, she's doing everything that we never did. Why? Poor Charles is having such a hard time.' Meanwhile, he decided he couldn't suggest too much. Wasn't his place to advise her.

I suppose I did [worry about William], with Harry it wasn't so bad [the morning sickness]. With William it was appalling, almost every time I stood up I was sick. But that was a combination, I couldn't define which was which or what triggered it off but obviously I felt it was a nuisance to the set-up and I was made to feel it was a nuisance to the set-up. Suddenly in the middle of a black dress and black tie do, I would go out to be sick and come back again and they'd say: 'Why didn't she go off to bed?' I felt it was my duty to sit at the table, duty was all over the shop. I didn't know which way to turn at all.

I threw myself down the stairs [at Sandringham]. Charles said I was crying wolf and I said I felt so desperate and I was crying my eyes out and he said: ' I'm not going to listen. You're always doing this to me. I'm going riding now.' So I threw myself down the stairs. The Queen comes out, absolutely horrified, shaking – she was so frightened. I knew I wasn't going to lose the baby; quite bruised around the stomach. Charles went out riding and when he came back, you know, it was just dismissal, total dismissal. He just carried on out of the door.

Birth of William

When we had William we had to find a date in the diary that suited him and his polo. William had to be induced because I couldn't handle the press pressure any longer, it was becoming unbearable. It was as if everybody was monitoring every day for me. Anyway we went in very early. I was sick as a parrot the whole way through the labour, very bad labour. They wanted a Caesarean, no-one told me this until afterwards. Anyway, the boy arrived, great excitement. Thrilled, everyone absolutely high as a kite – we had found a date where Charles could get off his polo pony for me to give birth. That was very nice, felt very grateful about that! Came home and then postnatal depression hit me hard and it wasn't so much the baby that had produced it, it was the baby that triggered off all else that was going on in my mind. Boy, was I troubled. If he didn't come home when he said he was coming home I thought something dreadful had happened to him. Tears, panic, all the rest of it. He didn't see the panic because I would sit there quietly.

[At William's christening] I was treated like nobody else's business on 4th August [1982]. Nobody asked me when it was suitable for William – 11 o'clock couldn't have been worse. Endless pictures of the Queen, Queen Mother, Charles and William. I was excluded totally that day. I wasn't very well and I just blubbed my eyes out. William started crying too. Well, he just sensed that I wasn't exactly hunky-dory.

Royal life

When I first arrived on the scene I'd always put my head down. Now that I interpret it that it did look sulky. I've never sulked. I've been terrified out of my tiny little mind. I never sulked as child, it's just not in me. I was just so frightened of the attention I was getting, it took me six years to get comfortable in this skin and now I'm ready to go forward.

One minute I was nobody, the next minute I was Princess of Wales, mother, media toy, member of this family, you name it, and it was too much for one person at that time.

Basically my husband's office got in a turmoil because one minute there was one and the next minute there were two and the presents coming in from the wedding were so phenomenal – from a swimming pool, to a desk set, to a photograph frame to six dining-room chairs. Chaos! I ended up writing my own thank-you letters.

Edward Adeane [Prince Charles's private secretary from 1979–85] was wonderful – we got on so well. Very much the bachelor and I was always trying to find him the ideal woman but I didn't succeed at all. He said: 'I know some nice ladies who might be ladies-in-waiting. Will you come and see them and meet them?' So I said 'Yes' to them all, even though I didn't really know them and one or two have gone by the wayside but the others have remained very strong and I've gathered a few on the way as well.

What I can remember is that I didn't want to do anything on my own. I was too frightened. The thought of me doing anything on my own sent tremors, so I stuck with whatever Charles did. If that included a wife I went with him all the way – wherever. But the pace was phenomenal. I knew I couldn't do engagements as well as get married, plus doing up two houses.

Building up her wardrobe

On the day we got engaged I literally had one long dress, one silk shirt, one smart pair of shoes and that was it. Suddenly my mother and I had to go and buy six of everything. We bought as much as we thought we needed but we still didn't have enough. Bear in mind you have to change four times a day and suddenly your wardrobe expands to something unbelievable. Hence, probably, the criticism when I first arrived on the scene of having new clothes all the time. Three seasons and I had to deck myself out from January to December overnight with hats, gloves, the lot. After that I asked Anna Harvey from *Vogue*, where both my sisters had worked, to come and help me out with the basic things like two of this, three of this, one of that. But after that I was on my own. Once I got established names like Victor Edelstein and Catherine Walker I could do it myself, ring them up and talk to them. But, before then, Anna definitely helped out for the first year. I had to find a niche where I was happy with the designer and what I required. I couldn't have fashionable clothes because it wouldn't have been practical for the job but I had to have clothes that had to last all day long, sensible colours and sensible neckline and skirt length. I never knew a thing about having weights in hems [to prevent skirts from blowing up in the wind]. I found it all out in my own time. No-one helped with that.

First royal engagements

[One of] the very first royal ones was with Liz Taylor called *The Little Foxes*. It was a play. I remember I turned up in a fake white fur coat and all the antis came out against me for evermore. So that went back into the cupboard, never to be seen again. I was pregnant with William and it was agonizing because I didn't find Elizabeth Taylor very easy to talk to.

[On switching on the Regent Street Christmas lights] I remember wearing a pair of navy blue culottes with a pink shirt and I felt so sick. I couldn't do them up because I was pregnant but I didn't have anything else to wear. And I was so nervous. I had to make a speech in front of the whole of Regent Street. I was shit scared.

It didn't get easier – I just got used to what people required from the Princess of Wales. What Diana thought wasn't going to come into it – yet. I hadn't got enough background on what the Princess of Wales was supposed to do. I could adapt but it took some time.

I went to Hereford [SAS headquarters] and did a driving course. Bombs were being thrown at me. It was terrifying. Graham Smith was my first policeman who came from Princess Anne. He'd been with her a few years. He was sweet but it took a long time to get used to having a policeman – God, suddenly to have this man in your car, music had to be turned down, I had to make sure he was fed, all those things which you don't have to do, but I was brought up to look after others.

The first overseas tour

Then it was make-or-break time for me. We went to [Australia and] New Zealand, Alice Springs. This was the real hard crunch, the hard end of being the Princess of Wales. There were thousands of press following us. We were away six weeks and the first day we went to this school in Alice Springs. It was hot, I was jet-lagged, being sick. I was too thin. The whole world was focusing on me every day. I was in the front of the papers. I thought that this was just so appalling, I hadn't done something specific like climb Everest or done something wonderful like that. However, I came back from this engagement and I went to my lady-in-waiting, cried my eyes out and said: 'Anne, I've got to go home, I can't cope with this.' She was devastated, too, because it was her first job. So that first week was such a traumatic week for me, I learned to be royal in inverted commas in one week. I was thrown into the deep end. Now I prefer it that way. Nobody ever helped me *at all*. They'd be there to criticize me, but never there to say 'Well done.'

When we came back from our six-week tour I was a different person. I was more grown up, more mature, but not anything like the process I was going to go through in the next four or five years. Basically our tour was a great success. Everybody always said when we were in the car 'Oh, we're in the wrong side, we want to see her, we don't want to see him,' and that's all we could hear when we went down these crowds and obviously he wasn't used to that and nor was I. He took it out on me. He was jealous; I understood the jealousy but I couldn't explain that I didn't ask for it. I kept saying you've married someone and whoever you'd have married would have been of interest for the clothes, how she handles this, that and the other, and you build the building block for your wife to stand on to make her own building block. He didn't see that at all.

The first foreign trip we took William to Australia and New Zealand. That was for six weeks. That was great – we were a family unit. It was very tricky, mentally, for me, because the crowds were just something to be believed. My husband had never seen crowds like it and I sure as hell hadn't and everyone kept saying it will all quieten down when you've had your first baby, and it never quietened down, never.

We never had a fight [about taking Prince William on tour]. The person who never got any credit was Malcolm Fraser who was then Prime Minister [but wasn't by the time of the tour]. He wrote to us out of the blue. All ready to leave William. I accepted that as part of duty, albeit it wasn't going to be easy. He wrote to me and said: 'It seems to me that you being such a young family would you like to bring your child out?' and Charles said: 'What do you think about this?' I said: 'Oh, it would be absolutely wonderful.' He said: 'Then we can do six weeks instead of four and we can cover New Zealand as well so it would be perfect.'

I said: 'Wonderful.' It was always reputed that I had had an argument with the Queen. We never even asked her, we just did it. It was very nice. We didn't see very much of him [William] but at least we were under the same sky, so to speak. That was a great fulfilment for me because everyone wanted to know about his progress.

Other foreign trips

President and Mrs Göncz of Hungary, I had an instant rapport with them. I got out of the aeroplane and we held hands. Extraordinary, it felt so normal me doing it. It was the story with all the papers at home. I remember thinking 'What's so odd about that?' It all got very intense after that with the public. Sudden shifts but I couldn't understand it. I had no-one to talk to about that with. I just thought I was growing up. Put it down to experience.

I thought that was rather wonderful, very special [an audience with Pope John Paul II]. I was totally overwhelmed. I was so intimidated by the set-up, we sat there with this man in a white frock. It was quite strange. I said one thing to him. I plucked up courage and said 'How are your wounds?' He had recently been shot. He thought I was talking about my womb! So he thought I was having a baby! So after that mistake I went very quietly.

In Spain I wasn't well at all, tiredness, exhaustion, bone tired. I told everybody I was tired but it was the bulimia taking a grip of me. Portugal was the last time we were close as man and wife. That's going back six or seven years ago now. Then Majorca [on holiday with the King and Queen of Spain], the first trip I spent my whole time with my head down the loo. I hated it so much. Because they were all so busy thinking Charles was the most wonderful creature there's ever been and who was this girl coming along? And I knew there was something inside me that wasn't coming out and I didn't know how to use it, in the sense of letting them see it. I didn't feel at all comfortable in that situation.

Christmas at Sandringham

It was fairly fraught. Isn't that awful? I can't remember what people bought me. I do all the presents and Prince Charles signs the cards. [It was] terrifying and so disappointing. No boisterous behaviour, lots of tension, silly behaviour, silly jokes that outsiders would find odd but insiders understood. I sure was [an outsider].

Trooping the Colour

Everybody mingles around. Those who want to talk to each other talk, those who don't don't. There are too many of us.

The birth of Harry

Then between William and Harry being born it is total darkness. I can't remember much, I've blotted it out, it was such pain. However, Harry appeared by a miracle. We were very, very close to each other the six weeks before Harry was born, the closest we've ever, ever been and ever will be. Then suddenly as Harry was born it just went bang, our marriage, the whole thing went down the drain. I knew Harry was going to be a boy because I saw on the scan. Charles always wanted a girl. He wanted two children and he wanted a girl. I knew Harry was a boy and I didn't tell him. Harry arrived, Harry had red hair, Harry was a boy. First comment was 'Oh God, it's a boy', second comment 'and he's even got red hair'. Something inside me closed off. By then I knew he had gone back to his lady but somehow we'd managed to have Harry. Harry was a complete joy and is actually closer to his father than perhaps William at the moment.

Prince Charles went to talk to my mother at Harry's christening and said: 'I'm so disappointed – I thought it would be a girl.' Mummy snapped his head off, saying 'You should be thankful that you had a child that was normal.' Ever since that day the shutters have come down and that's what he does when he gets somebody answering back at him.

Relations with the royal family:

The Queen

The relationship certainly changed when we got engaged because I was a threat, wasn't I? I admire her. I long to get inside her mind and talk to her and I will. I've always said to her 'I'll never let you down but I cannot say the same for your son.' She took it quite well. She does relax with me. She indicated to me that the reason why our marriage had gone downhill was because Prince Charles was having such a difficult time with my bulimia. She saw it as the *cause* of the marriage problems and not a symptom. I kept myself to myself. I didn't ask her advice. Now I can do it myself.

I get on very well with them [her parents-in-law] but I don't go out of my way to go and have tea with them.

Prince Charles

[I was] accused very early on of stopping him shooting and hunting – that was total rubbish. He suddenly went all vegetarian and wouldn't kill. His family thought he had gone mad, and he was ostracized within the family. They couldn't understand it and they were fearful of the future – all the estates have things that need to be shot on them. So if the heir wasn't going to take an interest, panic was going to set in. It was an influence well before me, but it all came back eventually in his own time. He does that – he has these crazes and then he drops them.

[Charles's clothes] He had an awful lot but he had very little. For instance, he had ghastly Aertex pyjamas that were honestly, simply hideous, so I bought him a silk pair, that sort of thing – and shoes. Yes, they were well received. He was absolutely thrilled.

[Charles as a father] He loved the nursery life and couldn't wait to get back and do the bottle and everything. He was very good, he always came back and fed the baby. I [breast] fed William for three weeks and Harry for eleven weeks.

Queen Mother

[The Queen Mother's 90th birthday] Grim and stilted. They are all anti me. My grandmother [Ruth, Lady Fermoy] has done a good hatchet job on me.

Prince Philip and Prince Charles

Very tricky, very tricky. Prince Charles longs to be patted on the head by his father while father longing to be asked advice instead of Prince Charles giving advice.

Prince Andrew

Andrew was very, very noisy and loud. It occurred to me that there was something troubling him. He wasn't for me. Andrew was very happy to sit in front of the television all day watching cartoons and videos because he's not a goer. He doesn't like taking exercise – he loves his golf and it's rather touching. But he gets squashed by his family the whole time. He's dismissed as an idiot but actually there's a lot more that hasn't arisen yet. He's very shrewd and astute.

Sweet Koo adored him. She was terribly good to have around. Very gentle and looked after him. Very quiet, devoted all her energies to him. Suited each other so well. Met her lots of times.

Princess Anne

We're always supposed to have had this tricky relationship. I admire her enormously. I keep out of her way but when she's there I don't rattle her cage and she's never rattled mine and the fuss about her being godmother to Harry was never even thought about. I thought to myself 'There's no point having anyone in the family as godparents as they are either aunts or uncles.' I said: 'The press will go for that,' and Charles said: 'So what?' They had this great thing about she and I not getting on. We get on incredibly well, but in our own way. I wouldn't ring her up if I had a problem, nor would I go and have lunch with her but when I see her it's very nice to see her. Her mind stimulates me, she fascinates me, she's very independent and she's gone her own way.

Other royals

I've always adored Margo [Princess Margaret], as I call her. I love her to bits and she's been wonderful to me from day one. Everyone keeps themselves to themselves. The Gloucesters – they are a very shy couple anyway. Feel sorry for her [the Duchess of Kent]. Would look after her if I had to.

Diana's mother and the royal family

Whenever I mention my mother's name within the royal family, which I barely do, they come on me like a ton of bricks. So I can never do anything in that department. They're convinced she's the baddie and that poor Johnnie [her father] had a very rough time.

Years of suffering

I think an awful lot of people tried to help me because they saw something going wrong but I never leant on anyone. None of my family knew about this at all. Jane, my sister, after five years of being married, came to check on me.

I had a V-neck on and shorts. She said: 'Duch [Diana's childhood nickname], what's that marking on your chest?' I said: 'Oh, it's nothing.' She said: 'What is it?' And the night before I wanted to talk to Charles about something. He wouldn't listen to me, he said I was crying wolf. So I picked up his penknife off his dressing table and scratched myself heavily down my chest and both thighs. There was a lot of blood and he hadn't made any reaction whatsoever.

[On other suicide attempts] I was running around with a lemon knife, one with the serrated edges. I was just so desperate. I knew what was wrong with me but nobody else around me understood me. I needed rest and to be looked after inside my house and for people to understand the torment and anguish going on in my head. It was a desperate cry for help. I'm not spoiled – I just needed time to adapt to my new position.

I don't know what my husband fed her [the Queen]. He definitely told her about my bulimia and she told everybody that was the reason why our marriage had cracked up because of Diana's eating and it must be so difficult for Charles.

It was at the Expo [in Canada] where I passed out. I remember I had never fainted before in my life. We'd been walking round for four hours, we hadn't had any food and presumably I hadn't eaten for days beforehand. When I say that, I mean food staying down. I remember walking round feeling really ghastly. I didn't dare tell anyone I felt ghastly because I thought they'd think I was whinging. I put my arm on my husband's shoulder and said: 'Darling, I think I'm about to disappear,' and slid down the side of him. Whereupon David Roycroft and Anne Beckwith-Smith [royal aides] who were with us at the time took me to a room. My husband told me off. He said I could have passed out quietly somewhere else, behind a door. It was all very embarrassing. My argument was I didn't know anything about fainting. Everyone was very concerned. I fainted in the American section. While Anne and David were bringing me round, Charles went on around the exhibition. He left me to it. I got back to the hotel in Vancouver and blubbed my eyes out. Basically I was overtired, exhausted and on my knees because I hadn't got any food inside me. Everyone was saying: 'She can't go out tonight, she must have some sleep.' Charles said: 'She must go out tonight otherwise there's going to be a sense of terrific drama and they are going to think there's something really awful wrong with her.' Inside me I knew there was something wrong with me but I was too immature to voice it. A doctor came and saw me. I told him I was being sick. He didn't know what to say because the issue was too big for him to handle. He just gave me a pill and shut me up.

It was all very strange, I just felt miserable. I knew the bulimia started the week after we got engaged. My husband put his hand on my waistline and said: 'Oh, a bit chubby here, aren't we?' and that triggered off something in me – and the Camilla thing, I was desperate, desperate.

I remember the first time I made myself sick. I was so thrilled because I thought this was the release of tension. The first time I was measured for my wedding dress I was 29 inches around the waist. The day I got married I was 23½ inches. I had shrunk into nothing from February to July. I had shrunk to nothing.

On the outside, people were saying I gave my husband a hard time, that I was acting like a spoilt child, but I knew I just needed rest and patience and time to adapt to all the roles that were required of me overnight. By then there was immense jealousy because every single day I was on the front of the newspapers. I read two newspapers, albeit I was always supposed to have read them all. I did take criticism hard because I tried so hard to show them that I wasn't going to let them down, but obviously that didn't come across strongly enough at that point. We had a few trying to cut wrists, throwing things out of windows, breaking glass. I threw myself downstairs when I was four months pregnant with William, trying to get my husband's attention, for him to listen to me.

But he just said, 'You're crying wolf.'

I gave everybody a fright. I couldn't sleep, I just never slept. I went for three nights without any sleep at all. I had no fuel to sleep on. I thought my bulimia was secret but quite a few of the people in the house recognized it was going on, but nobody mentioned it. They all thought it was quite amusing that I ate so much but never put any weight on.

I always kept my breakfast down. I don't know what the hell it was. I didn't keep vitamin pills. I just got help from somewhere – I don't know where it came from. I swam every day, I never went out at night, I didn't burn candles at both ends. I got up very early in the morning, on my own, to be on my own and at night-time went to bed early, so it wasn't as though I was being a masochist to my system but not to my energy level. I always had terrific energy, I've always had.

It went on and on. Only a year and half ago I suddenly woke and realized that I was on the way down fast. I just cried at every opportunity which thrilled people in a way because when you're crying in this system you are weak and 'Good, we can handle it.' But when you bounce up again, 'What the hell has happened?' questions again.

The public side was very different from the private side. The public side, they wanted a fairy princess to come and touch them and everything will turn into gold and all their worries would be forgotten. Little did they realize that the individual was crucifying herself inside, because she didn't think she was good enough. 'Why me, why all this publicity?' My husband started to get very jealous and anxious by then, too. Inside the system I was treated very differently, as though I was an oddball and I felt I was an oddball, and so I thought I wasn't good enough. But now I think it's good to be the oddball, thank God, thank God, thank God!

I had so many dreams as a young girl that I wanted, and hoped this that and the other, that my husband would look after me. He would be a father figure and he'd support me, encourage me, say 'Well done,' or say 'No, it wasn't good enough,' but I didn't get any of that. I couldn't believe it, I got none of that, it was role reversal.

He [Prince Charles] ignores me everywhere. Ignored everywhere and have been for a long time but if people choose to see that now they are a bit late in the day. He just dismisses me.

[The worst day of my life] was realizing that Charles had gone back to Camilla.

[On her feelings of isolation] Definitely separation from friends. I would be too embarrassed to ask them to come in for lunch. I couldn't cope with that. I would be apologizing the whole way through lunch.

Fergie

I met Fergie when Charles was getting near me and she kept rearing her head for some reason and she seemed to know all about the royal set-up, things like that. She just sort of encouraged it. I don't know, she just suddenly appeared and she sat in the front pew of our wedding – and everything like that. She came to lunch at Buckingham Palace and didn't seem daunted by it all.

I wasn't quite sure how to take it. Suddenly everybody said: 'Oh, isn't she marvellous, a breath of fresh air, thank God she's more fun than Diana.' So Diana was listening and reading every line. I felt terribly insecure. I thought maybe I ought to be like Fergie and my husband said: 'I wish you would be like Fergie – all jolly. Why are you always so miserable? Why can't you be like Grannie? Why can't you be like Grannie?' I'm quite glad I'm not Grannie now. I made so many balls-ups trying to be like Fergie. I went to a pop concert, Spider concert, David Bowie, with David Waterhouse and David Linley. David Linley was on my right and David Waterhouse on my left. I went in leather trousers which I thought was the right thing to do, completely putting out of mind that I was the future Queen and future Queens don't wear leather like that in public. So I thought that was frightfully 'with it', frightfully pleased to act my own age. Slapped hands. The same summer at Ascot I put a brolly up somebody's backside. In my astrological chart Penny Thornton always said to me: 'Everything you will do this summer you will pay for.' I did, definitely. I learnt a lot.

I got terribly jealous and she got terribly jealous of me. She kept saying to me 'You mustn't worry, Duch, everything is going to be fine, let me do this, let me do that.' I couldn't understand it, she was actually enjoying being where she was, whereas I was fighting to survive. I couldn't understand how she could find it so easy. I thought she would be like me and put her head down and be shy. No, a different kettle of fish altogether and she wooed everybody in this family and did it so well. She left me looking like dirt.

But up in Scotland she used to do everything that I never did. So I thought, 'This can't last, the energy of this creature is unbelievable.' Meanwhile everybody looking at me – 'It's a pity Diana has gone so introverted and quiet, she was so busy and trying to sort herself out,' and then this holocaust arrived. I knew eventually she would turn round and say 'Duch, how on earth have you survived all these years?' She's said it now for the last two years. I never explain. I just say it's just happened.

The turning-point [in Klosters, Switzerland in 1988]

We went off skiing. I had flu, I had been in bed for two days. Third day in bed. Fergie came back in the afternoon at 2.30 pm. She was carrying Beatrice then, she was four to five months pregnant. She landed upside-down in a ditch and had come back shaken, pale and exhausted. I put her to bed and both of us were in the chalet and we heard this helicopter go up. I said to her: 'There's been an avalanche,' and she said: 'Something's gone wrong.'

We heard Philip Mackie [royal aide] come into the chalet. He didn't know that the two girls were upstairs. We heard him say: 'There's been an accident,' so I shouted down: 'Philip, what's going on?' 'Oh, nothing at all, nothing at all, we'll tell you soon.' I said: 'Tell us now.' He said: 'There's been an accident and one of the party is dead.' So we sat there, we just sat on top of the stairs, Fergie and I, and we didn't know who it was.

Half an hour later it came through that it was a man and then three-quarters of an hour later Charles rang up Fergie to tell her that it wasn't him, that it was Hugh [Major Hugh Lindsay, a former equerry to the Queen]. That really turned me inside out. So everyone started shaking. They didn't know what to do next. I said to Fergie: 'Right, we must go upstairs and pack Hugh's suitcase and do it now while we don't know what's hit us. We must take the passport out and give it to the police.' And we went upstairs and packed everything. I took the suitcase downstairs and said to Tony [Prince Charles's bodyguard]: 'I've put the suitcase under your bed. It's there when you need it but we'd like Hugh's belongings back so we can give them to Sarah [Major Lindsay's wife], his signet ring, his watch.' I felt terribly in charge of the whole thing. I said to my husband: 'We're going home, to take the body home to Sarah, we owe it to Sarah to take the body home.' Anyway, there were tremendous arguments about that. I got my policeman to get Hugh's body out of the hospital.

Anyway, so we came back from Klosters. We arrived back at Northolt and we had Hugh's coffin in the bottom of the aeroplane and Sarah was waiting at Northolt, six months pregnant and it was a ghastly sight, just chilling. We had to watch the coffin come out and then Sarah came to stay with me at Highgrove when I was on my own and she cried from dawn to dusk and my sister came and every time we mentioned the name of Hugh, there were tears, tears, but I thought it was good to mention his name because she had to cleanse herself of it, and her grief went long and hard, because he was killed in a foreign country, she wasn't out there with him, they'd only been married eight months, she was expecting a baby. The whole thing was ghastly and what a nice person he was. Out of all the people who went it should never have been him.

Fergie and I were closer to Hugh than Charles. He was very good with all the members of my husband's family, he always was a star trouper.

I took charge there. My husband made me feel so inadequate in every possible way that each time I came up for air he pushed me down again and when my bulimia finished two years [ago] I felt so much stronger mentally and physically so was able to soldier on in the world. Even if I ate a lot of dinner Charles would say: 'Is that going to reappear later? What a waste.' He talked to my sister about it and said: 'I'm worried about Di, she's not sleeping, can't you talk to her?' I suppose he's worked it out.

Long road to recovery

I think the bulimia actually woke me up. I suddenly realized what I was going to lose if I let go and was it worth it? Carolyn Bartholomew rang me up one night and said: 'Do you realize that if you sick up potassium and magnesium you get these hideous depressions?' I said: 'No.' 'Well, presumably that's what you suffer from, have you told anyone?' I said: 'No.' 'You must tell a doctor.' I said: 'I can't.' She said: 'You must, I'll give you one hour to ring up your doctor and if you don't I'm going to tell the world.' She was so angry with me, so that's how I got involved with the shrink called Maurice Lipsedge. He came along, a sweetheart, very nice. He walked in and said: 'How many times have you tried to do yourself in?' I thought, 'I don't believe this question,' so I heard myself say 'Four or five times'. He asked all these questions and I was able to be completely honest with him and I spent a couple of hours with him and he said: 'I'm going to come and see you once a week for an hour and we're just going to talk it through.' He helped me get back my self-esteem and he gave me books to read. I kept thinking 'This is me, this is me, I'm not the only person.'

Dr Lipsedge said: 'In six months' time you won't recognize yourself. If you can keep your food down you will change completely.' I must say it's like being born again since then, just odd bursts, lots of odd bursts, especially at Balmoral (very bad at Balmoral) and Sandringham and Windsor. Sick the whole time. Last year it was once every three weeks whereas it used to be four times a day and it was a big 'hooray' on my part. My skin never suffered from it nor my teeth. When you think of all the acid! I was amazed at my hair.

I hated myself so much I didn't think I was good enough, I thought I wasn't good enough for Charles, I wasn't a good enough mother – I mean doubts as long as one's leg.

I've got what my mother's got. However bloody you're feeling you can put on the most amazing show of happiness. My mother is an expert at that. I've picked it up, kept the wolves from the door but what I couldn't cope with in those dark ages was people saying, 'It's her fault.' I got that from everywhere,

everywhere, the system, and the media started to say it was my fault – 'I was the Marilyn Monroe of the 1980s and that I was adoring it.' I've never *ever* sat down and said: 'Hooray, how wonderful,' never, because the day I do that we're in trouble in this set-up. I am performing a duty as the Princess of Wales as my time is allocated. If life changes, it changes but at least when I finish, as I see it, my 12 to 15 years as Princess of Wales . . . I don't see it any longer funnily enough.

From day one, I always knew I would never be the next Queen. No-one said that to me – I just knew it. I got an astrologist in six years ago. 'I've got to get out, I can't bear it any longer,' and she said to me: 'One day you will be allowed out but you will be allowed out as opposed to divorcing or something like that.' It always sat in my mind, she told me that in 1984, so I've known it for some time.

There was no praise, I would go for dinner and he would say: 'Oh, not that dress again,' or something like that, but one of the bravest moments of my entire ten years was when we went to this ghastly party for Camilla's sister's 40th birthday party. Nobody expected me to turn up but again a voice inside me said: 'Go for the hell of it.' So I psyched myself up something awful. I decided I'm not going to kiss her, shake her hand instead. And I was feeling frightfully brave and bold and basically Diana's going to come away having done her bit. He needled me the whole way down to Ham Common where the party was. 'Oh, why are you coming tonight?' – needle, needle, needle, the whole way down. I didn't bite but I was very, very on edge.

Anyway, I walk into the house and stick my hand out to Camilla for the first time and think 'Phew, I've got over that.' We all sat down and, bearing in mind they were all my husband's age, I was a total fish out of water but I decided I am going to try my hardest. I was going to make an impact.

And then after dinner we were all upstairs and I was chatting away and suddenly noticed there was no Camilla and no Charles upstairs. So this disturbed me, so I make my way to go downstairs. I know what I'm going to confront myself with. They tried to stop me from going downstairs. 'Oh, Diana, don't go down there.' 'I'm just going to find my husband, I would like to see him.' I had been upstairs about an hour and a half so I was entitled to go down and find him. I go downstairs and there is a very happy little threesome going on downstairs – Camilla, Charles and another man chatting away. So I thought 'Right, this is your moment,' and joined in the conversation as if we were all best friends and the other man said: 'I think we ought to go upstairs now.' So we stood up and I said: 'Camilla, I'd love to have a word with you if it's possible,' and she looked really uncomfortable and put her head down, and I said to the men: 'Boys, I'm just going to have a quick word with Camilla,' and 'I'll be up in a minute,' and they shot upstairs like chickens with no heads, and I could feel upstairs all hell breaking loose. 'What's she going to do?'

I said to Camilla: 'Would you like to sit down?' So we sat down and I was terrified and I said: 'Camilla, I would just like you to know that I know exactly what is going on between you and Charles, I wasn't born yesterday.' Someone was sent down to relieve us, obviously, 'Go down there, they're having a fight.' It wasn't a fight – calm, deathly calm and I said to Camilla: 'I'm sorry I'm in the way, I obviously am in the way and it must be hell for both of you but I do know what is going on. Don't treat me like an idiot.' So I went upstairs and people began to disperse. In the car on the way back my husband was over me like a bad rash and I cried like I have never cried before – it was anger, it was seven years' pent-up anger coming out. I cried and cried and cried and I didn't sleep that night. And the next morning when I woke up I felt a tremendous shift. I'd done something, said what I felt, still the old jealousy and anger swilling around, but it wasn't so deathly as before, and I said to him at the weekend three days later: 'Darling, I'm sure you'll want to know what I said to Camilla. There's no secret. You may ask her. I just said I loved you – there's nothing wrong in that.' I said: 'That's what I said to her, I've got nothing to hide, I'm your wife and the mother of your children.'

That was it, it was a big step for me.

I was desperate to know what she said to him – no idea of course! He told a lot of people the reason why the marriage was so wobbly was because I was being sick the whole time. They never questioned what it was doing to me.

[Diana's sister] Jane's wonderfully solid. If you ring up with a drama, she says: 'Golly, gosh, Duch, how horrible, how sad and how awful' and gets angry. But my sister Sarah swears: 'Poor Duch, such a shitty thing to happen.' My father says: 'Just remember we always love you.'

But that summer [1988] when I made so many cock-ups I sat myself down in the autumn, when I was in Scotland, and I remember saying to myself: 'Right, Diana, it's no good, you've got to change it right round, this publicity, you've got to grow up and be responsible. You've got to understand that you can't do what other 26- and 27-year olds are doing. You've been chosen to do a position so you must adapt to the position and stop fighting it.' I remember my conversation so well, sitting by water. I always sit by water when contemplating.

Stephen Twigg [a therapist] who comes to see me said once: 'Whatever anybody else thinks of you is none of your business.' That sat with me. Then once someone said to me, when I said I've got to go up to Balmoral, and they said: 'Well, you've got to put up with them but they've also got to put up with you.' This myth about me hating Balmoral – I love Scotland but just the atmosphere drains me to nothing. I go up 'strong Diana'. I come away depleted of everything because they just suck me dry, because I tune in to all their moods and, boy, are there some undercurrents there! Instead of having a holiday, it's the most stressful time of the year. I love being out all day. I love the stalking.

I'm much happier now. I'm not blissful but much more content than I've ever been. I've really gone down deep, scraped the bottom a couple of times and come up again and it's very nice meeting people now and talking about tai-chi and people say: 'Tai-chi – what do you know about tai-chi?' and I said: 'An energy flow,' and all this and they look at me and they say: 'She's the girl who's supposed to like shopping and clothes the whole time. She's not supposed to know about spiritual things.'

At the Aids hospice last week [July 1991] with Mrs Bush was another stepping stone for me. I had always wanted to hug